## Picture credits:

t:top, b:bottom, m: middle, l: left, r: right and c: centre

Cover tr: NASA images

6tr: NASA images, 13br: Everystockphoto [A. Belani],
21br: imagesofasia.com, 23tr: Wikimedia Commons, 24tr: Wikimedia
Commons, 25tl: Wikimedia Commons, 25mr: Wikimedia Commons,
27br: Everystockphoto[ja_macd], 31tl: NASA images, 31ml: NASA
images, 31br: NASA images, 33tr: Wikimedia Commons,
33br: Everystockphoto[dullhunk], 34mr: earlytelevision.org,
35tl: Wikimedia Commons, 36tl: Wikimedia Commons,
36mr: Wikimedia Commons, 38br: Everystockphoto[Stahlkocher],
40mc: Everystockphoto[guldfisken]
Back cover tl: 38br: Everystockphoto[Stahlkocher]

### Design and Research:

Netscribes (India) Pvt Ltd

### Published By:

North Parade Publishing Ltd.,
4 North Parade, Bath, BA1 1LF UK

# Contents

# Invention vs Discovery

Invention is to create something which never existed before. Discovery is to find information about a place or object which was previously unknown, but was always there.

The history of human civilisation is full of daring explorers. Some shoot up to the sky, some dive deep into the sea, all in search of knowledge.

NASA X-43

Inventors are knowledge-seekers who usually spend their time in laboratories. Innovation relates to new ideas or methods.

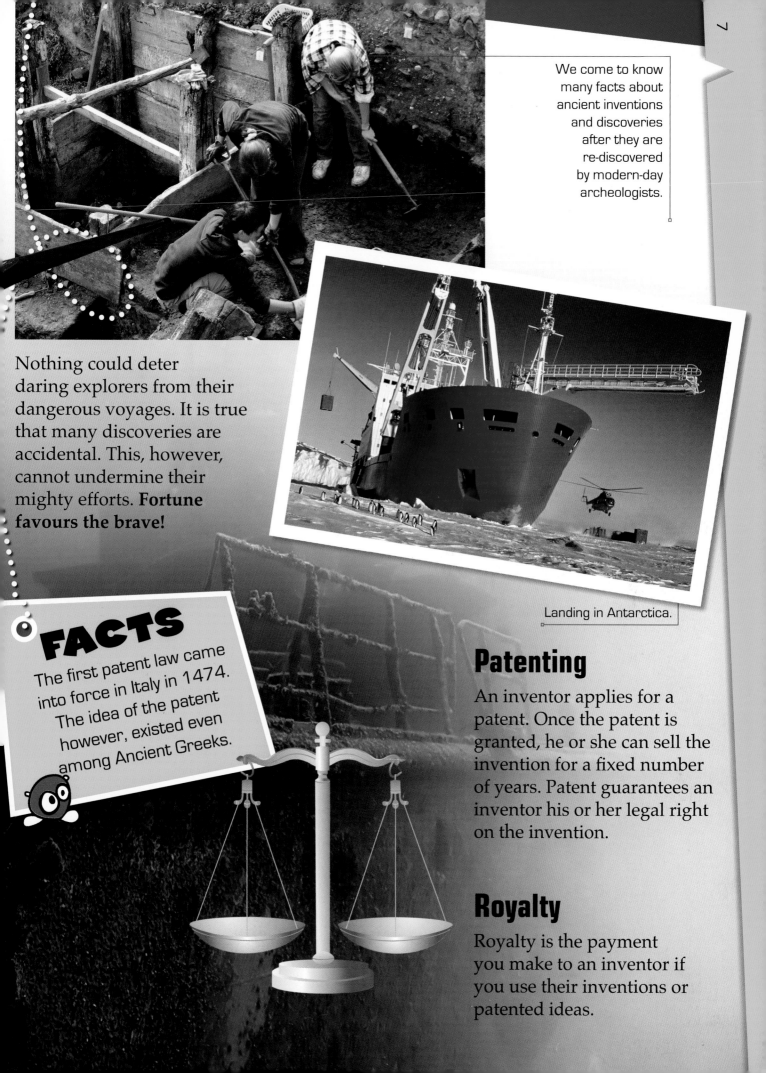

We come to know many facts about ancient inventions and discoveries after they are re-discovered by modern-day archeologists.

Nothing could deter daring explorers from their dangerous voyages. It is true that many discoveries are accidental. This, however, cannot undermine their mighty efforts. **Fortune favours the brave!**

Landing in Antarctica.

# FACTS

The first patent law came into force in Italy in 1474. The idea of the patent however, existed even among Ancient Greeks.

## Patenting

An inventor applies for a patent. Once the patent is granted, he or she can sell the invention for a fixed number of years. Patent guarantees an inventor his or her legal right on the invention.

## Royalty

Royalty is the payment you make to an inventor if you use their inventions or patented ideas.

# Prehistoric Times

Nobody can tell for sure the exact dates of different inventions in a period which does not have written records of their achievements. We usually put them under one umbrella: prehistoric inventions.

## Fire

A long time ago, prehistoric humans learnt to make fire by striking two stones against each other. The friction caused sparks, which eventually turned to flames. Slowly, they learnt to cook food and heat up their dens in winter. Life became easier. Fire was invented in about 10,000 BC.

## Seeds

Humans started growing plants by sowing seeds in 10,000 BC. As they learnt the basics of farming, their nomadic nature changed. They started settling down in one place.

The history of civilisation began with the invention of fire.

# Pottery

Pre-historic humans learnt to make pottery by making rings of clay. They used a circular base on which they placed the dough of clay and made the rings with both hands. They baked the clay rings in the fire.

# Bow and Arrow

Bows and arrows were the earliest forms of weapons that humans used for hunting. They invented bows and arrows in about 15,000 BC.

The arrows often had barbed tips.

The early bows were made of wood.

# Needle and Thread

Needle and thread was another interesting invention of the prehistoric age. The needles were usually made of bones or ivory. They used the tendons of animals and horsehair as threads. Needles and threads were available as early as 15,000 BC!

# Stonehenge

Stonehenge in England was built in 5000–3000 BC. This also marks the first use of tools e.g. antlers of red deer were used for architectural purposes.

# FACTS

Tattoos! Pre-historic people started decorating their bodies with naturally available ochre and iron oxide as early as 400,000 years ago. To make up the colours, they invented grinding machines.

WOW!!!

# Weaving

It's thought women of the early periods invented weaving. In the prehistoric days, people weaved reeds to make small containers like our modern day baskets.

Part of Stonehenge — the first astronomical observatory, measuring the rising and setting positions of the sun and planets.

# Ancient Egypt

Mummies and pyramids pop up in our minds with the very mention of Ancient Egypt. There are many other amazing facts about this ancient civilisation.

## Papyrus

The idea of paper we use to write on came to the Egyptians for the first time. They learnt to use the fibre of papyrus plants to make paper.

## Sails

Egypt is famous for the Nile River. Hence, the idea of water transport should have come to them quite early. They invented sails to be used in boats and ships.

## First Ox-Drawn Plow

Plowing of land began with the ox-drawn plow. The Egyptians invented it in 2,500 BC. Ever since then, humans have cultivated their own food.

# Hieroglyphics

They also invented the early writing system in the form of Hieroglyphics. Papyrus and Hieroglyphics greatly helped

# Shadoof

Shadoof is another of the Egyptians' amazing inventions. It helped them in irrigating their fertile lands. They used it to collect water from large water bodies, like the Nile, and used the same on agricultural lands.

Egypt also developed the first leap year calendar in 238 BC.

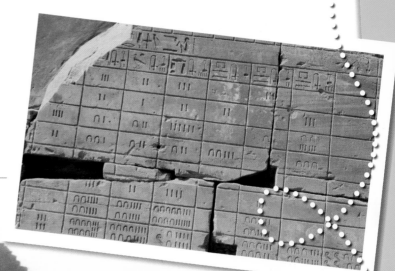

Highly organised work forces made these constructions possible.

# 365 Day Calendar and Leap Year

The idea of a 365 day scientific date calendar occurred for the first time in Ancient Egypt.

# Organised Labour

Ancient Egypt is known for its marvellous pyramids. Such huge structures were possible only after they conceived organised labour. Many people worked for several decades to complete each of the pyramids!

## FACTS

We owe a number of household objects to the people Ancient of Egypt. They invented scissors, locks and even the air cooling system.

GREAT!

# Mesopotamia

Modern day Iraq and parts of Iran, Syria and Turkey formed ancient Mesopotamia. The Mesopotamians consisted of the Sumerians, the Babylonians and the Assyrians. The Sumerians were the earliest inhabitants of Mesopotamia.

## Chariots

Chariots are a Mesopotamian invention. This made transport easy. Chariots were also used in warfare.

## Glazed Brick

Glazed bricks of different colours were a special feature of Mesopotamian architecture. The famous Ishtar Gate of Babylon has the finest use of their invention.

Mesopotamian Chariot.

Backgammon originated in Mesopotamia.

# 360 Degrees

As the Mesopotamians learnt to divide a circle into 360 degrees, timekeeping and geometry took new turns.

# FACTS

The Mesopotamians used a calculating system based on 60, which later gave us the idea of hours, minutes and seconds.

THANK YOU!

# Battering Ram

Early Mesopotamian soldiers invented battering rams to break through enemy walls. This was highly useful while invading another territory.

# Game of Checkers

People in Mesopotamia revelled in indoor games. The earliest checker board dates back to 3,000 BC. This was found in Ur, Iraq.

Hammurabi – the earliest written law code.

# Seeder Plow

The seeder plow, an early Mesopotamian invention, made it possible to simultaneously plow a land and sow seeds in the furrows. There are mythological stories about its origin.

# Hammurabi's Law

Hammurabi was the ruler of Babylon, an ancient city of Mesopotamia. He introduced Hammurabi's Law — the earliest written codes in the history of law.

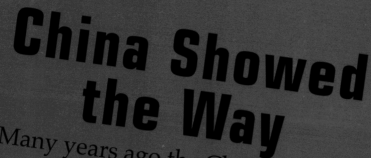

# China Showed the Way

Many years ago the Chinese people invented a way to locate directions. They made the first compass made up of a square metal plate and a ladle-shaped loadstone. China has countless other contributions that took civilisations forward.

## Fireworks

China made the world's first fireworks. They filled bamboo tubes with gunpowder. Then they applied fire to it, producing flare and motion.

## Paper

Ts'ai Lun invented paper in AD 104 in China. He used the inner bark of a mulberry tree, bamboo fibre and water to make a pulp which, when flattened and dried, became paper.

Ancient Chinese people making bamboo pulp that then would be spread on a piece of rough cloth. As the water drained through the cloth, it left a flat coarse sheet of paper.

## Abacus

China offered the first counting machine — the abacus. They used beads and wires. The modern day computer is the lineal descent from this five thousand-year-old invention!

2+2=?

## Porcelain

Tao-Yue invented porcelain. He used white clay or kaolin, easily found along the banks of Yangzte river, to make the same.

Porcelain – the finest chinaware.

## FACTS

The Chinese people made the first kite out of silk and bamboo.

## Woodblock Printing

Woodblocks dipped in ink and pressed against a piece of cloth marks the earliest form of printing. Later, people replaced cloth with paper. The first book printed by this method dates back to AD 868. It was called *Diamond Sutra*.

## Fork

People in China eat with chopsticks. But long before they invented chopsticks, they used forks made of bones (2400–1900 BC). The Chinese were the first to use forks for eating!

Text and images were carved on blocks of wood

## Gunpowder

In the ninth century, a Chinese monk mixed saltpeter with sulphur. This was an accidental discovery but soon became a regular weapon in warfare.

# The Greeks— Mapping History

The Greeks not only showed the world how to make amazing buildings, they also led the way in map making and geometry.

## Coins and Propaganda

Western Turkey, erstwhile Lydia, saw the birth of coins. However, the Greeks used text or images on such coins to spread opinions or glory.

## Maps

Anaximander, in Greece, made the world's first map. He made a world map along with 26 regional maps and 67 local maps. He lived between 610 to 546 BC.

## Theatre

Ancient followers of Greek god Dionysus played mythological satyrs through songs and dance. In 500 BC, a priest called Thespis replaced songs with prose. This came to be known as the first Greek tragedy and marked the beginning of theatre.

This is where they played the famous tragedies.

# Pythagoras' Theorem

Pythagoras was a Greek mathematician from the fifth century BC. He discovered that in a right-angled triangle, the square of the longest arm of the triangle, known as hypotenuse, is equal to the square of the other two arms put together.

A Greek catapult.

# Abax

The Greeks spread sand on a table top and used it to make geometric designs. They also carved lines on table tops and used it as a counting tool. Pebbles were the counting units. This device is called Abax.

# Catapult

Around 400 BC, the Greeks invented catapults. They used the first catapults to shoot heavy arrows at enemies.

# Archimedes' Screw

Archimedes' screw is not the same screw we use to join things together. This screw can be used to draw water from a low-lying source to higher planes. Archimedes made his first screw in 300 BC.

## FACTS

Whoooa!

The Greeks invented hula hoops. They used bamboo, wood, even grass or vines to make hula hoops.

# Mighty Rome

Ancient Rome is not all about gladiators and chariot races. They made some of the most useful inventions that we still use today.

## Glassblowing

Before glassblowing, glass making was an expensive process. Only rich people could afford to use glass. As the Romans started the process of glassblowing, using glassmakers from foreign lands, glass became affordable to all.

## Cement

Ancient Romans made the first cement for construction purposes. They added pozzolanic to traditional mortar and made cement out of the mix.

## Aqueducts

The Romans invented aqueducts to supply water to the cities. Many cities still use aqueducts built with the Ancient Roman technique. The Romans made eleven aqueducts between 312 BC and 226 BC.

## Bridges

Ancient Romans made large, long-lasting bridges.

## FACTS

*WOW!*

Ancient Romans invented cranes to lift huge objects.

## Dams

Dams were erected in Ancient Rome often to support pleasure lakes. They were the first to make dams and people still find them useful in different parts of the world.

## Modern Roads

Modern roads and tunnels are based on the Ancient Roman model. The Romans pioneered road construction which was later followed by other parts of the world.

## Amphitheatres

Amphiteatres for sport and entertainment are a Roman concept. Gladiators fought here.

The Colosseum, the earliest amphitheatre, can be seen in Rome today.

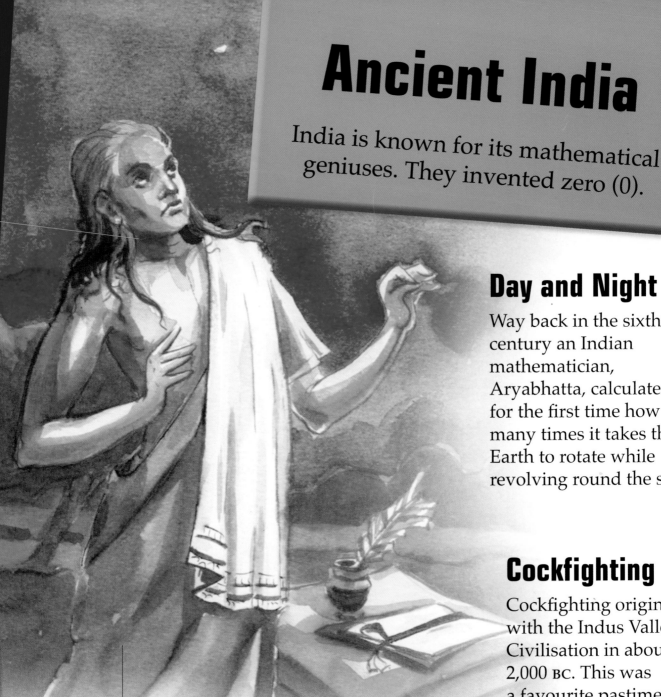

# Ancient India

India is known for its mathematical geniuses. They invented zero (0).

## Day and Night

Way back in the sixth century an Indian mathematician, Aryabhatta, calculated for the first time how many times it takes the Earth to rotate while revolving round the sun.

Aryabhatta taught us how eclipses are caused.

## Cockfighting

Cockfighting originated with the Indus Valley Civilisation in about 2,000 BC. This was a favourite pastime for the Indus Valley people.

## Ruler

Indus Valley, an ancient civilisation based in India, used rulers for measurement for the first time.

Cockfighting is now illegal in many countries.

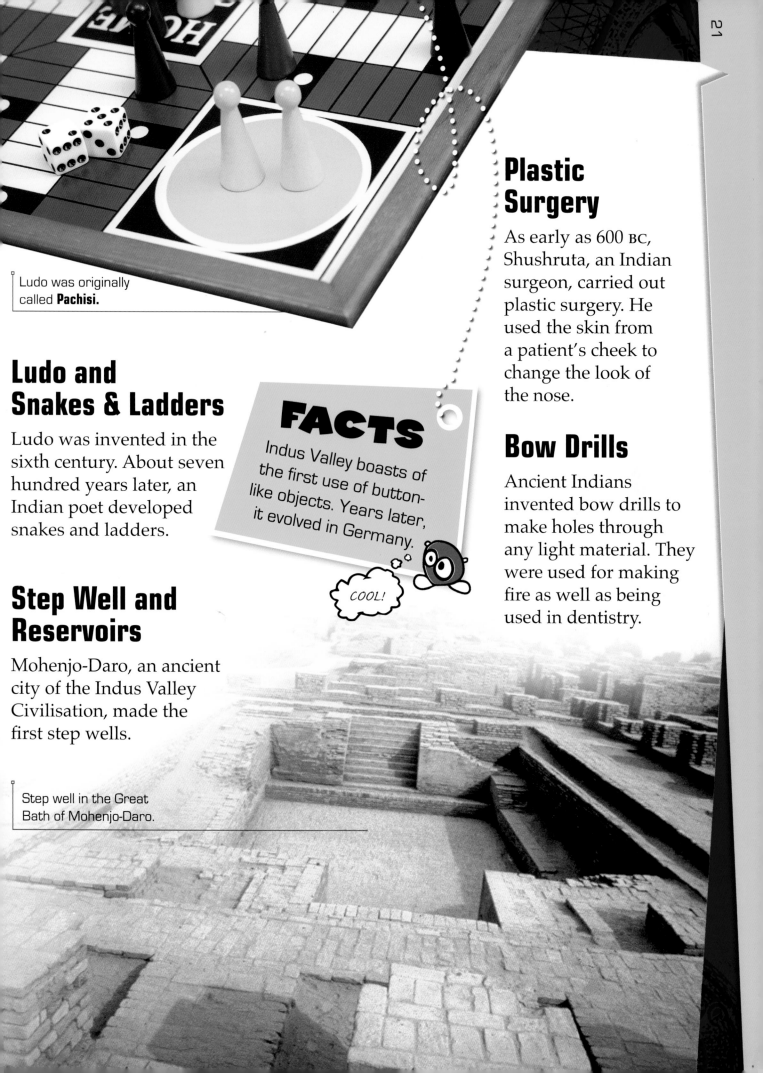

Ludo was originally called **Pachisi.**

# Ludo and Snakes & Ladders

Ludo was invented in the sixth century. About seven hundred years later, an Indian poet developed snakes and ladders.

# Step Well and Reservoirs

Mohenjo-Daro, an ancient city of the Indus Valley Civilisation, made the first step wells.

Step well in the Great Bath of Mohenjo-Daro.

## FACTS

Indus Valley boasts of the first use of button-like objects. Years later, it evolved in Germany.

*COOL!*

# Plastic Surgery

As early as 600 BC, Shushruta, an Indian surgeon, carried out plastic surgery. He used the skin from a patient's cheek to change the look of the nose.

# Bow Drills

Ancient Indians invented bow drills to make holes through any light material. They were used for making fire as well as being used in dentistry.

# Native America

There was an America much before Christopher Columbus discovered it. It was inhabited by Native Americans. They made many remarkable inventions.

## Freeze-Drying

The Inca people used to store their crops on high mountains where it is very cold throughout the year. This marked the beginning of the freeze-drying of food.

## Mayan Calendar

The Mayan calendar comprised 18 months of 20 days. It had five extra days added to make up a year.

*The Haab* or civil calendar was invented by the Mayans.

## Terrace Farming

The first evidence of terrace farming is found in Peru, where the Incas lived.

Terrace farming relics from ancient Peru.

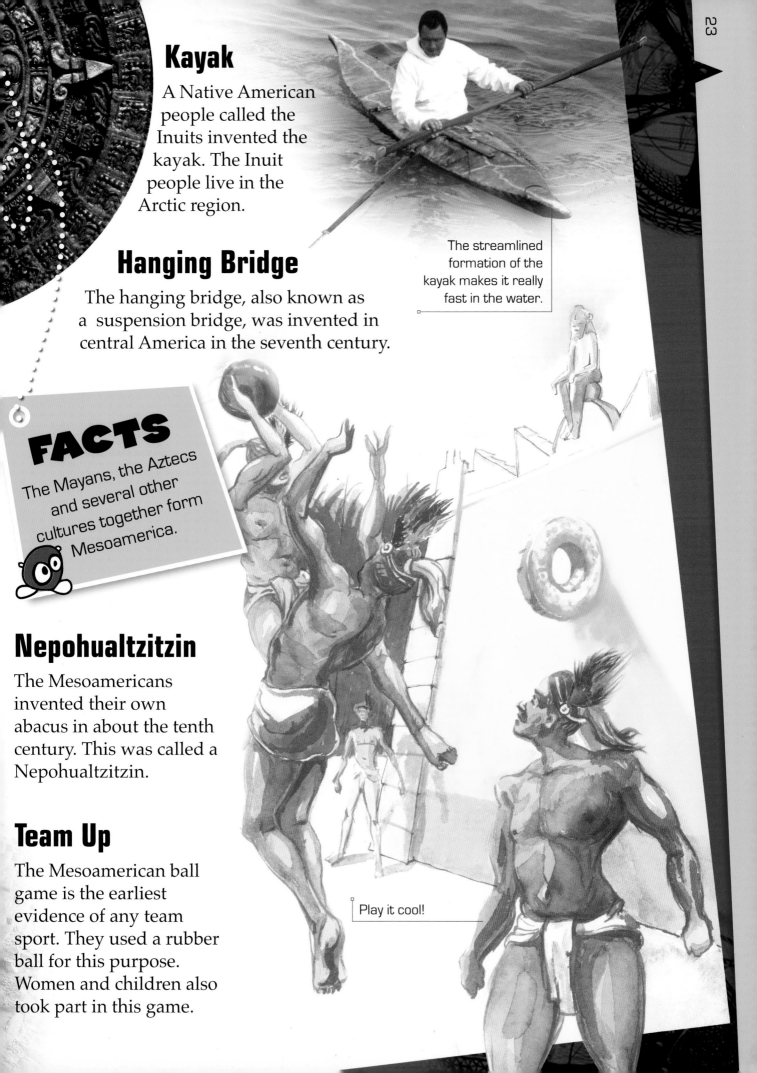

# Kayak

A Native American people called the Inuits invented the kayak. The Inuit people live in the Arctic region.

The streamlined formation of the kayak makes it really fast in the water.

# Hanging Bridge

The hanging bridge, also known as a suspension bridge, was invented in central America in the seventh century.

## FACTS

The Mayans, the Aztecs and several other cultures together form Mesoamerica.

# Nepohualtzitzin

The Mesoamericans invented their own abacus in about the tenth century. This was called a Nepohualtzitzin.

# Team Up

The Mesoamerican ball game is the earliest evidence of any team sport. They used a rubber ball for this purpose. Women and children also took part in this game.

Play it cool!

# Daring Explorers!

The thirteenth to sixteenth century is marked with a series of discoveries. Many new lands and trade routes opened up to people all over the world.

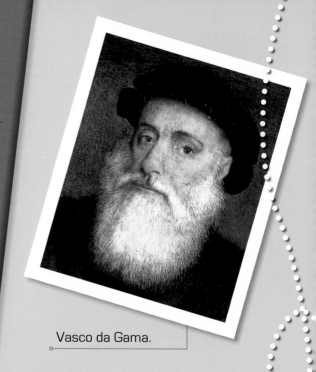

Vasco da Gama.

## Jacques Cartier

Jacques Cartier was a French explorer who discovered the region known today as Canada.

## Vasco da Gama

Vasco da Gama discovered the sea route from Europe to India. Exploring this sea route was also the ambition of his father Estavao. He could not make it though.

Marco Polo and his silk route.

## FACTS

The Silk Route is the route that separates China from Europe and west Asia. It was the most dangerous trade route of the Middle Ages.

## Marco Polo

Marco Polo was the first person from the West to travel across China, India and Sri Lanka. He was a guest of Kublai Khan for seventeen years.

Marco Polo set out on the journey to China: 1271

Christopher Columbus discovered America: 12 October 1492

Vasco Da Gama reached India: 20 May 1498

Magellan's ship, Victoria, reached Spain on 6 September 1522.

## Magellan

Ferdinand Magellan's ship, Victoria, was the first to successfully sail around the world. However, he died before his ship reached home. He was killed by the native people of the Philippines.

Francisco Pizarro.

Columbus was an Italian Spanish explorer.

# Christopher Columbus

Christopher Columbus set out to find a direct route from Europe to Asia. He never reached Asia, but accidentally found a new land which came to be known as America.

## Cortes

Hernan Cortes, a Spanish explorer, discovered Mexico in the early sixteenth century. This brought Mexico under Spanish rule.

## Pizarro

Francisco Pizarro discovered South America. He also established Lima, the capital city of Peru. Fransisco Pizarro's father was a second cousin to Hernan Cortes!

Hernan Cortes reached Mexico: March 1519

Ferdinand Magellan set out on his tour: 10 August 1519

Jacques Cartier discovered Canada: 1534

Fransisco Pizarro founded Lima: 18 January 1535

# The Period of Darkness

The Middle Ages, often called the Dark Ages, saw some remarkable inventions. It was not that dark after all!

Tick tock! Telling time since the Middle Ages.

## Mechanical Clock

Early mechanical clocks were used in monasteries. The clock had bells that tolled the hour to call the monks to prayer.

## Tidal Mill

People in the Middle Ages built tidal mills in coastal areas. Those tidal mills captured water energy to grind grains.

## Windmill

Primitive windmills existed in 200 BC. By about AD 1100, they assumed the shape we recognise today. The Middle Age Europeans used windmills to grind corns. The Dutch used them to drain out water during floods.

Nature provides power, no cost involved!

# Hourglass

An hourglass has two glass bulbs joined vertically by a very narrow neck. The top part is filled with sand in such a way that it takes exactly one hour for the sand to trickle down completely to the lower bulb.

Top Bulb

Neck

Lower Bulb

# Oars

The invention of oars brought in massive changes in water transport.

## FACTS

Eyeglasses were invented in the thirteenth or fourteenth century in Europe.

# Blast Furnace

Blast furnaces were invented sometime around AD 1100. They are used to extract metals from their ores.

# Spinning Wheel

The first ever mechanized form of spinning wheel, an apparatus for spinning yarn or thread, was invented in the Middle Ages in Europe.

A spinning wheel from the Middle Ages.

# Towards Enlightenment

The Dark Ages started a process of scientific research which ushered in a new age — the Renaissance. Exact periodic distinction between the two ages often gets blurred.

## Microscope

Microscopes came into use in late sixteenth-century England. Marcello Malpighi, Robert Hooke and Antoni va Leeuwenhoek made significant contributions to its development.

A simple microscope.

## FACTS

William Harvey of England discovered the workings of blood circulation in the human body. He also described how the heart pumps blood to maintain the circulatory system.

Gutenberg's printing machine and a page from the Gutenberg Bible – the first book it printed.

## Printing Press

Though the Ancient Chinese people taught how to print, Johannes Gutenberg of Germany established the first printing press in 1436. He used moveable types for printing.

AND in the I. yere vppon the euen of Sainct Thomas the Apostle before Christmas, was yelden by appoinct ..to the castle of Kenelworthe. ..be the king with his ..is said;

## First Use of Compass in Navigation

Though compasses were invented before the Middle Ages, they were first used in 1405 for navigational purposes.

A seventeenth century Navigator compass.

An antique globe.

## Telescope

Hans Lippershey, originally a German lens maker who later moved to the Netherlands, invented the telescope in 1608.

## Globe

Martin Behaim made the first globe in 1492. He was a German navigator and merchant.

## Astrolabe

The theoretical origin of astrolabes dates back to Ancient Greece, but its truly practical usage started in fourteenth-century England.

Nicolus Copernicus holding an astrolabe.

## Earth's Magnetic Field

William Gilbert, a noted physician of the late sixteenth century, first pointed out that the Earth is a huge magnet!

# Exploring the Sky

Even the sky isn't the limit...

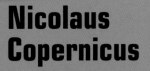

## Nicolaus Copernicus

Nicolaus Copernicus, a Polish astronomer, used mathematical calculations to establish the idea of the Solar System.

Nicolus Copernicus.

Galileo Galilei.

## Galileo

Galileo Galilei made a telescope thirty times more powerful than that of Hans Lippershey. With this telescope he discovered four natural satellites of Jupiter in 1610.

## Isaac Newton

Isaac Newton established the fact that any two objects on earth apply gravitational forces on each other. And this law extends to anywhere in the universe.

Sir Isaac Newton.

## Halley's Comet

Edmund Halley studied Newton's laws carefully. Using these laws, he calculated that it takes 76 years for Halley's Comet to be seen from Earth. Halley's Comet will be seen next in 2061.

Copernicus completed his heliocentric theory: 1543

Galileo discovered satellites of Jupiter: 1610

Launch of Sputnik I and II: 1957

# Yuri Gagarin

On 12 April 1961, Yuri Gagarin, a Russian cosmonaut, set out in a spacecraft Vostok I. He was the first man ever to travel in space and also encircle the Earth along its orbit.

Gagarin during Vostok launch.

## FACTS

Yuri Gagarin died in a plane crash. He and his instructor Vladimir Seryogin were flying a MiG 15UTI aircraft when the accident took place.

OH NO!

# Sputnik

Russia sent the first ever artificial satellites that travelled round the Earth. They are called Sputnik I and Sputnik II. Sputnik II carried Laika, a dog. It is the first living being to travel in space.

Sputnik I.

Astronaut Edwin Aldrin on the Lunar Surface. Photograph taken by Neil Armstrong.

# Men on the Moon

Commander Neil Alden Armstrong and Lunar Module Pilot Edwin Eugine Aldrin Jr. were the first humans to walk on the Moon. The mission was called Apollo 11.

Launch of Vostok I: 12 April 1961

Armstrong and Aldrin Jr reached Moon: 20 July 1969

Launch of first reusable spacecraft: 1981

Hubble Telescope orbited: 1990

# Health is Wealth

There was a time when people looked to supernatural forces for the cause of any disease. However, with advances in medicine and health care, doctors now look for the natural causes of a disease and treat people accordingly.

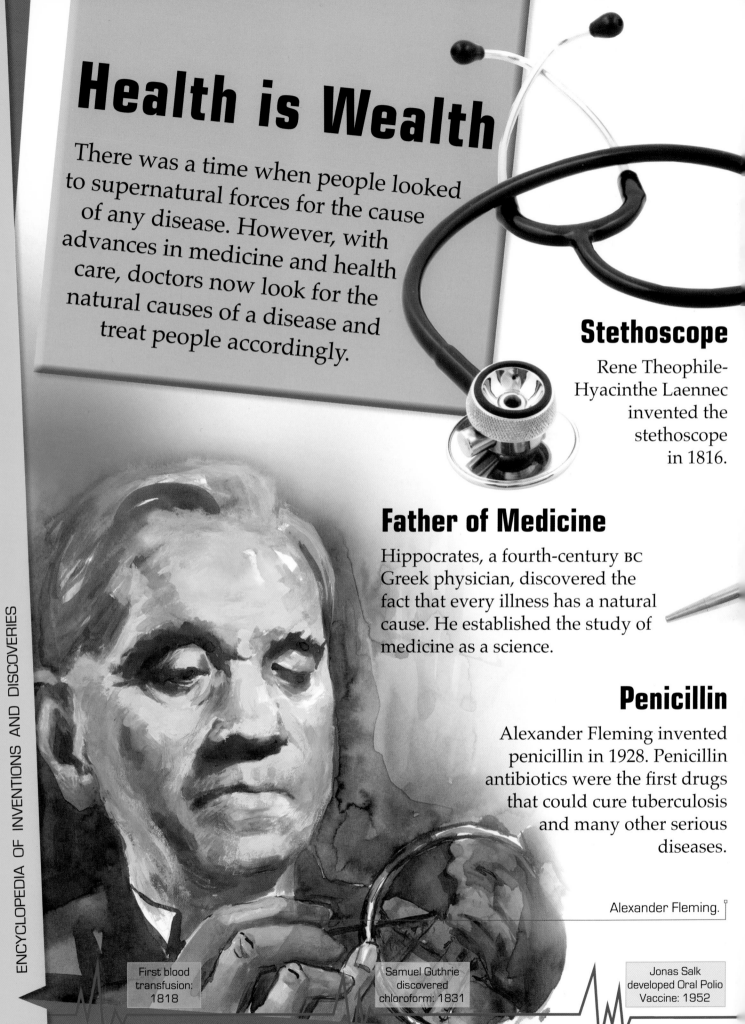

## Stethoscope

Rene Theophile-Hyacinthe Laennec invented the stethoscope in 1816.

## Father of Medicine

Hippocrates, a fourth-century BC Greek physician, discovered the fact that every illness has a natural cause. He established the study of medicine as a science.

## Penicillin

Alexander Fleming invented penicillin in 1928. Penicillin antibiotics were the first drugs that could cure tuberculosis and many other serious diseases.

Alexander Fleming.

First blood transfusion: 1818

Samuel Guthrie discovered chloroform: 1831

Jonas Salk developed Oral Polio Vaccine: 1952

# CAT or CT Scan

South African physicist Allan Cormack and British engineer Godfrey Hounsfield invented the CT scan in 1972. CT scanning is used to take pictures of the brain. This invention earned both of them the Nobel Prize in 1979.

The prototype CT scanner.

# Syringe

Gabriel Pravaz and Alexander Wood invented the hypodermic needle — a hollow pointed needle — in 1853.

A metal syringe.

# Anaesthesia

The invention of anaesthesia in the 1840s saved patients from terrible pain during surgery.

GREAT!!

# FACTS

Worldwide, there about 3,500 heart transplants carried out every year!

Sculpture of Edward Jenner at the Great Manchester Museum.

# First Vaccination

Doctors often inject germs of a disease in us. This in turn, makes us fortified against more dangerous forms of the same disease. This is called vaccination. Edward Jenner, an English doctor, invented this process in the late eighteenth century.

Louis Pasteur and Robert Koch proved the germ theory of disease: 1870

Launch of Hepatitis B Vaccine: 1981

First full face transplant operation by Laurent Lantieri: 2008

# Communication

The Romans invented the postal service in AD 14. Paper, the printing press and many other inventions improved communication systems over the centuries. However, the real surge in technology came about in the twentieth century.

Baird's television apparatus.

## Radio

Guglielmo Marconi, an Italian scientist, invented the radio. He conducted the first successful radio communication in 1902.

## Telephone

Alexander Graham Bell invented the telephone in 1876.

Alexander Graham Bell.

## Television

On 23 Janurary 1926, John Logie Baird came up with the world's first mechanical television apparatus. Philo T. Farnsworth invented an image dissector in 1927 which stands as a milestone in the history of television.

Charles Babbage presented Difference Engine: 14 June 1822

Konrad Zuse invented Z1: 1936

Konrad Zuse invented Z3: 1941

John Presper Eckert & John W. Mauchly made ENIAC: 14 February 1946

Charles Babbage's difference engine – an invention that made him the Father of Computing.

## Internet

An English scientist, Timothy Berners-Lee, invented the World Wide Web in 1989. The original use of the World Wide Web was to share information among a group of scientists scattered across the globe but who were working for the same organisation.

## Computer

Charles Babbage created the first basic design for a computer. Konrad Zeus invented Z3 — the world's first fully automatic computing machine — in 1941.

## Mobile Phone

On 3 April 1973, Dr Martin Cooper invented mobile phones. His first generation or 1G phones gave way to much more advanced 3G mobiles in 2003.

## FACTS

Guglielmo Marconi used the iron-mercury-iron coherer with a telephone detector for his successful experiment. This coherer was invented by Sir J. C. Bose, an Indian scientist, in 1898!

Bluetooth – a wireless mode of data transfer.

## Bluetooth

Jaap Haartsen and Sven Mattisson invented Bluetooth technology in 1994. Bluetooth was introduced to the market in 1998.

## Walkie-talkie

Donald L. Hings developed walkie-talkies for the Canadian soldiers during World War II. Later, people started using walkie-talkies for commercial purposes.

Walkie-talkie.

UNIVAC, first commercial computer: 1951

First computer game: 1962

Douglas Engelbert invented the first computer mouse: 1964

First personal computer, Apple II, launched: 1977

# Energy

We need energy to perform any work. Energy is available in different forms. Heat, light and sound are some of those forms.

Benjamin Franklin.

## Electricity

Ancient Greeks invented electricity. However, it had to wait till 1831 when Michael Faraday invented the electric dynamo for its regular use in technology.

## Lightning and Electricity

Benjamin Franklin established the relation between lightning and electricity while he was flying a kite during a thunderstorm. Eventually, he invented the electric rod.

Thomas Edison.

## Steam

Thomas Savery and Thomas Newcomen are a few of the pioneers in the research related to steam and its use. However, James Watt ushered in a whole new era with his invention of the steam engine.

## Bulb

Thomas Alva Edison made the first electric bulb using carbon filament on 22 October 1879.

## Hydrothermal Power

The first hydrothermal power plants were established in the late nineteenth century. A hydrothermal power plant converts water to steam and produces electricity.

Solar panel.

## Wind Turbine

Though the history of windmills dates back to antiquity, the first automatic wind turbine was built in Cleveland. Charles F Brush owns the credit. He installed it in 1888.

Wind turbine.

## FACTS

Charles Fritts invented solar cells in 1883. Since the electric current generated from each solar cell is very low, they are arranged in a series to form a solar panels.

## Electromagnets

Hans Christian Oersted discovered the fact that electric current, if passed through certain metals, can turn the metal into a magnet. Following this research, William Sturgeon invented artificial magnets or electromagnets in 1823.

# Moving Ahead!

The saga of land transport began with the invention of the wheel. Sumerian chariots rolled out the trend of human carriers, which culminated in the latest sophisticated trains and cars.

Early bicycle.

## Coaches

The first four-wheeled coaches were made in Hungary in the sixteenth century.

Early steam coach.

## Bicycle

Kirkpatrick Macmillan of Dumfriesshire, Scotland, was a blacksmith by profession. He invented the bicycle in 1839.

## First Car

Nicolas Joseph Cugnot invented the car in 1769. Henry Ford's Model T, originally priced at $825, was the first affordable car that was made available to the public.

Model T 1911.

Nicolas Cugnot made the first self-propelled car: 1769

Jean Joseph Étienne Lenoir made the first coal-gas engine: 1858

Louis Renault invented drum brakes: 1902

Ford Motor Company made the Model-T: 1908

# Steam Engines

Thomas Newcomen created the first successful steam engine in 1712. James Watt improved on this to make the first commercially successful steam engines in 1776. Richard Trevithick made the first steam locomotive in 1804.

A steam engine.

## FACTS

Maglev trains do not run on wheels. They use magnets instead. The first maglev train was introduced in 1979 in Germany.

*That's Great!*

# Diesel Engine

Rudolf Diesel built the prototype diesel engine in 1897. The first road vehicle to run on diesel was an agricultural tractor. Almost half the cars in Europe run on diesel these days.

# Electric Engine

Thomas Parker invented electric cars in 1884.

Monorails run on a single track attached to the ground.

# Monorail

In 1821, Henry Robinson Palmer conceived the idea. The first monorail carried passengers along the Chestnut line in Hertfordshire, England, in 1925.

Charles Kettering invented the electric starter motor: 1911

Power steering system introduced: 1926

Karl Pabst designed the Jeep: 1940

First hybrid engine: 1997

# Riders to the Sea

The invention of rafts signalled the simplest means of sea transport for the prehistoric people living by the sea. Slowly, it gave rise to many sophisticated vessels that we see around today.

## Rafts

Lieutenant John Fremont made the first rafting expedition on the Platte River in 1842. He used rubber, which was invented by Horace H. Day. In ancient times, people usually used logs, plants and reeds to make their simple rafts.

## Viking Ships

The Vikings moved in long narrow ships that were the fastest of their time. They invented the Viking ships in about AD 800.

Viking ships.

Roman battleship caught in a storm.

## Roman Battleships

After the Punic War, the Romans invented their own battleships based on the model of Carthaginian quinqueremes. This made the Roman Navy more powerful than ever.

William Borne designed the first submarine: 1578

Cornelis Drebbel built the first submarine: 1620

Robert Fulton made the Nautilus submarine: 1798

Petroleum and electric engine used in submarines: 1895

## Junk

These are early Chinese war boats. Chinese junks used multiple masts for the first time.

Junk: an early Chinese war boat.

## Spanish Armada

As the Spanish ruler planned to attack England in 1588, 34 warships were built for this purpose. This special purpose fleet of warships came to be known as the Spanish Armada.

## Luxury Liners

Luxury liners transport people from one port to another. The first luxury liner route started in 1818, between the UK and USA.

Travel in luxury.

## Submarines

Cornelius Jacobszoon Drebbel built the first submarine in 1620. The first submarine to be used in a battle was 'Turtle'. David Bushnell invented it in 1775.

A submarine surfacing above water.

## FACTS

Earlier wooden ships gave way to iron ships when Sir Anthony Deane first used iron in ship building in 1670.

GREAT!

First use of the diesel engine in submarines: 1904

First submarine with a snorkel mast: 1943

First nuclear powered submarine, USS Nautilus (SSN571) introduced: 1954

# The Sky is the Limit!

Conquering the sky has long been the dream of humans. The advent of balloons and different modern aircrafts turned this dream into a reality.

Replica of Wright Flyer, the first aeroplane.

## Wright Flyer

Orville and Wilbur Wright made the first aeroplane that successfully took to the sky. It is known as the Wright Flyer. Orville Wright piloted the aircraft for 12 seconds on 17 December 1903.

## Balloon

Joseph and Jacques Montgolfier successfully demonstrated the first balloon on 4 June 1783. By 15 October 1783, the Montgolfier brothers' balloon carried its first human passengers.

## Biplane

A biplane.

Biplanes have two sets of wings. The Wright Brothers made their first biplane in 1899. This was three years before the successful demonstration of the Wright Flyer.

First British Royal Engineers Balloon Unit: 1878

First bomber plane invented: 1912

First Zeppelin aircraft attack: October 1914

Spitfire fighter plane introduced: 1936

# Triplane

Triplanes have three sets of wings. Ambroise Goupy designed the first triplane in 1908.

A triplane ready to take off.

# Helicopter

Unlike other aircrafts that use fixed wings, helicopter wings rotate round a mast. Paul Cornu made the first helicopter in 1907 that was able to stay in the air for a considerable time. Paul Cornu was a French engineer.

A helicopter about to land.

# Modern Jetliner

Frank Whittle of England invented the jet engine in 1941. However, it took until 1948 for the first jet airliner (jetliner) called Vickers VC.1 Viking G-AJPH to be built.

Supersonic Jetliner, the fastest passenger aircraft.

# FACTS

Early passenger plane services were started by World War I veteran pilots. They started small companies after the War to offer civilian aviation services.

# Supersonic Jetliner

Concorde, the world's first supersonic jetliner, was first built by Anglo-French collaboration in 1969. Concorde was the fastest passenger aircraft.

| Mig-1 introduced: 1940 | Jet fighters introduced: 1944 | Air bombing on Hiroshima and Nagasaki: 1945 | Joint Strike Fighter came into use: 2001 |

# Glossary

**Amphitheatre**
Rows of seats arranged in a sloping manner around a flat ground where plays and sports were performed

**Astrolabe**
An instrument used to locate positions of the Sun, the Moon, stars and planets

**Astronaut**
One who travels in a spacecraft

**Astronomer**
One who studies the universe and heavenly bodies

**Catapult**
An instrument used to hurl objects at a great speed

**Comet**
A celestial body that moves round the Sun

**Commemorate**
To do something that will celebrate a person or an achievement for a long period of time

**CT Scan**
Computed tomography scan – a method used to take three dimensional pictures of the human body

**Culminate**
To reach the highest point

**Dentistry**
Treatment of people's teeth

**Explorer**
One who travels and discovers

**Fleet**
A group of ships

**Gladiators**
Ancient Roman fighters

**Hieroglyphic**
Written in a method where symbols and pictures are used instead of letters

**Hypotenuse**
The longest side of a right-angled triangle

**Kaolin**
A special type of white clay

**Locomotive**
Engine of a vehicle

**Navigation**
Deciding the direction of a ship, aeroplane, etc.

**Nomadic**
Moving from place to place and not having a permanent home

**Orbit**
The path through which a heavenly body moves around a planet or star

**Papyrus**
Tall plants that look like grass and grow in or near water

**Physician**
A medical doctor

**Pozzolan**
A material that gains cement-like properties when properly treated

**Prefabricated**
Objects that can be built from loose parts which can be assembled together

**Propaganda**
Spreading a message to influence people's opinion

**Renaissance**
Revival of interest in art, science, etc.

**Saga**
A long story about past achievements of people

**Satellite**
Any object moving around a bigger object in space

**Satyr**
A Greek god, half-man and half-goat in appearance

**Shadoof**
An ancient irrigation tool

**Stethoscope**
A medical instrument used to hear sounds from the chest or other parts of the body

**Theorem**
A mathematical statement or formula duly proved and accepted

**Tragedy**
A play about death or suffering

**Voyage**
A long journey

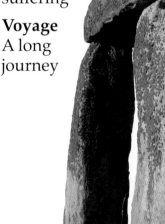

# Index